through winter

SÓLFJODUR

The Sólkráka Collective

THROUGH WINTER

epilogues

poems on the
ends of things

BEYOND

Mama, I am not afraid to die
never have been; you know why,
knew of it since I was five.
and though I love living all the same,
I know that somewhen, where, and day
the kindest heart will come for me.
I just hope she smiles,
grins and deems me an old friend,
a confidant, a good husband.
for if she frowns upon me,
if she sees me and feels doubt,
I'll have failed this life again.
And Mama, though I'm not afraid to die,
when off you go I do know I
will feel the loss for just a while.
but when you go, do so with ease,
for I promise that I will be
long behind though on the trail.
and for you I know he'll grin,
that softest-hearted gentleman
escorting you to your Beyond.

EPILOGUE

I remember seething,
hopes that I'd stop breathing,
desires to quell my heart from beating,
quietly repeating
things so self-defeating.
Joy was notwithstanding
Despair kept it sitting
merriment too fleeting
maybe I'd have died that
cold and lonesome evening;
all too many nearer-misses by Depression
left upon me cold and spiteful views, impression
that not even Death herself could ever want me
or that life was but a neverending taunting,
living was a task that always got more daunting
as increased the host that liked and likes to haunt me,
i faked many smiles (eyes were always gaunt
but shine a light or flicker, people never notice),
always think me happy, never see me joyless,
never took my quietude for sorrow, it's just
consequence of being some new kind of legend,

although precipices i was always edging,
going always closer
hear the wind keep howling
urging me to lie upon it, hear its growling
over me my melancholy liked to tower,
caught between a chasm and a field deflowered,
caught up in the hypnotism of a power
stronger than I was and many magnitudes more sour,
so I jumped and dove and fell and was submerged
'neath all the hatred of myself that had converged
and heard the heart there beating,
singing through the silence,
begging me to share with it a single ounce of kindness,
ounce is all I had, ounce is all heart's given,
but the song it sang kept many more within it,
one grew into three, and so my heart kept singing,
thanked me for the ounce of kindness I was lending,
repaid and shared one, such was the beginning
of the growth within me I'd been thinning, killing;
Heart and I started singing out together,
darkness couldn't gather, silence pierced and banished,
finding my own Heart relieved me of the famished
feeling I'd ignored for decade and a half
jokes my Heart would share
enticing me to laugh,
and how surprised was I
to hear the sound forsaken,
I had never thought from woe that I would break, yet
here I was defying,

Heart and I were crying,
I had thought it shattered,
always felt it dying —
maybe that's the notion
I had not envisioned,
ignored clearer vision, blew off the precision
required to recognise that always dying
means that I'm still living, somehow still trying,
and though they couldn't hear my endless crying,
my Heart always noticed,
always kept on drumming,
never stopped its goal of
one day maybe beating
murky sorrow, of one day just depleting
all of woe's resources,
shining as a beacon,
cutting off Despair's whole force
and thereby weaken
that cruel hindrance, that most
voracious vampire,
parasitic, venomous, dark empire,
remind me that light is something we can be, and
recollect the lumens bleeding out of me, sand
slips through fingers gathered altogether tightly,
rests in open palm: receive and hold as lightly
as required to inspire and aspire,
walk among the trees and revel in the sunlight,
expose heart to skies and seas and everlong expanses,
seek not happiness of others' half-full glasses,

look for love within, nourish the Heart that's singing,
pull yourself atop the precipice to which you're clinging
and rest awhile atop rocky spire,
ignore time limits, realise your desire
for the goodness, joy, and bliss cannot expire,
even at behest of those you might admire,
find in self that light which others see exuded,
recognise from expectation you're excluded,
grow despite the pressure from forces external
for it's solely you who has to deal eternal
with what you have done, and know that the infernal
is only that which you judge as such and return
to those moments in your youth where love was burning
brighter than the suns
created by your namesake,
recognise the lessons
learned from all your mistakes,
let go of the thought that you are somehow better,
improve self as often as deemed necessary
by the world with which you often fall in love
and roll with all the punches, let slide past the shoves,
recover as you're needing,
stop internal speeding,
recognise the blessings of the air that you're breathing;
Yes, I remember seething
hopes that I'd stop being;
now I find such mirth
in every single feeling,
stopped searching for love and ceased my expectation,

working on it always, forewent abnegation,
deem myself as worthy,
enjoy my existence,
reinforce my Heart against Despair's insistence,
recognise when I am tired and start resting,
friends and emperors stay nude but I am dressing,
keeping my own path despite others' suggestion,
utilising things and fighting 'gainst oppression,
knowing I have survived so much in short time-frame,
letting go instead of finding those to blame
for suffering and hurting as from those I've learned
so much about myself, so much of the world;
thankful for myself and thankful for divinity
and for the knowledge of self-love's infinity.
I'm onto the epilogue, now.

RAINBOW

final skies of evening blushing as they yawn
warmth of early morning's cloudy underbelly
Vincent's lovely dreaming, Summer's soft repose
life and verdant reaching, Nature's waxy fire
large and languid lakes, small echoes of the sea
(debated by science; as it returns, it leaves)
primal skies of nighttime as dear Luna dawns

CLOSING

what do you recall
as you near your end?
do you see the grins
of your dearest friends?
do you hear the cries
of so far away?

and let's say that you don't,
that you only see that day;
would you still choose to move on?
let's say that you won't,
is it here that you would stay,
or would you go on anyway?

can you feel it close;
does it pull away?
is it just a tug,
or a very subtle fade?
does it all turn bright
or dim like shade?

have you thought that you won't?
neither walk nor stray?
is it something you don't want,
or just some more to say?
you have a voice now;
use it before you—

SOFTEST MADNESS

it's a strange weakness,
a rising storm,
onwards struggle
keeping warm,
a vague notion
moving on.

what a soft madness,
restless embrace,
vision of sleeping,
open eyes, see your face
less a vision,
more a prayer,
hands clasped together,
lips to gods' ears;

what a strange weakness,
to only see
your eyes in water,
those storms at sea.
I should know better,
like how it ends,

with a slight whisper,
ruthless embrace,
your hand a summer,
your wounds a waste.
I'll breathe in seeds,
kisses like moss,
plant them on fissures,
break down the rocks.
make waste a beauty,
lichens dull the scars.
help guide your oceans
with warmer stars.

SHOALS

if life is but
dreams set upon different shores,
but bottles with paper
shut in with cork,
then released in waters,
cast out to the sea,
then I await greatly
for yours to meet me;
and if mine meet you
then 'tis merely returned
to hands, heart, and mind
for whom it always has burned,
a torch and a beacon
as old as our souls,
as old as these ghosts
found upon these dear shoals.

ON 8 FEBRUARY 2020, A CONSTELLATION RETURNED TO THE SKY

For Qing Han, the artist known as Qinni.
it's been such a year,
such an infinite time
since we first saw the art
of a heart so sublime.
it's hard to see stars
and not think oft of, too,
the nebulous beauty
handcrafted by you,
a vision so stellar, so strong
and still sad, a tinge
of melancholy oft to be had
by one whose own form
was so often at war,
an agony none of us
could have ignored —

yet you always kept fighting.
with your art you kept lighting
well past your penultimate day.

we miss you dearly, and wish you could have stayed.

TEMPUS MUNDI

well along the way,
must've realised the sun,
heard the softest of rays
falling and gracing
the side of your face,
and what stood there before us,
such wondrous vision,
led to pursuit of reason, of
kindness and merriment elusive and
so we give chase,

and though light flies above us,
and the caverns reach far below,
though to east lies the shoreline,
through us all the world does flow;

oh, can you hear the stars singing along,
only choruses, never alone,
so much light in the summer,
evenings filled with the hymns of insects;

oh, can you feel the moon humming,
smell the chill undulating along,
ground's so bright in the winter,
many lumens for frost to reflect;

oh, can you see the world grooving,
the vibrations both great and little,
spring's so joyous and yellow,
autumn's earthy and mellowly hued.

MOUNTAIN-CLIMBER

For Savannah Buik, 28 March 2018.
Mountain-climber, gone too high,
you've found yourself a place in sky,
and in our hearts, through which you fly
find peace, my friend; find peace.

Mountain-climber, gone too high,
amazed are we of you, and I —
though rarely near, my friend — yea, I
send peace, my friend; send peace.

Mountain-climber, gone too high,
whose mem'ries on the rock survive
and in our bluest skies shall thrive,
know peace, my friend; know peace.

Mountain-climber, gone too high,
our love for you shall never die
and though, to mourn, we all may cry,
find peace, my friend; find peace.

THE GRANDEST MOTHERS

For my grandmother, Mattie Green. 4 September 2021.

to my mighty protector,
loving, darling, ferocious,
unyielding and spacious
is her heart set for me.
oh, mighty protector,
to whom I cling dearly,
who lets me go wander
my eyes as the sea —
though my loving grandmother
passed days 'fore your party,
I have not lost a mother,
for joined you has she.

to she who made of me
a gift to my mother,
so gentle and gorgeous,
so sweet-smelling, ye.
oh, kindly gift-giver,
glitt'ring and honeyed,
who offers me beauty
every place I can see —
though my loving grandmother
passed days 'fore your party,
I have not lost a mother,
for joined you has she.

a song for every sun i've seen

HUMAN RACE

an atom reverberates, splits in twain,
an infinity later, becomes a brain,
implants itself, develops a spine,
sparks go flying, develops a mind,
mind generates, creates, prepares,
breaks down, overthinks, despairs,
sees and sees and wants and wants,
hears in darkness forever-taunts,
desires, desires, avariciously glares,
delights in having; if empty, swears,
directs gaze outwards, never does see
that garnering things makes not one free;
hands for grasping, hands to take,
hearts and arms and treaties to break,

mouth agape, eros demolished,
rights respecting lives abolished,
colours matter when upon skin,
genders, too, and cultures, then,
and where you're from, and what you do,
and if someone is just like you —
an atom splits, no echo there,
just one last sound.

HARRIET

brushing swiftly, sweeping off
the carcasses of fires past,
the desiccated logs rent into
shavings made of carbon, dust
in clouds always arising,
so dissimilar to what they were
mere hours past, yet warmth does linger
round, sensations of mirth and merriment
hovering much like a crowd,
gathered, perhaps, at her expense;
this wouldn't be the strangest thing.
she coughs; her throat has become dry.
hands on hips, she looks towards the sky.
she coughs again, using her forearm
to catch the horrid spray;
upon it is a wad of blood reminding her to stay.

HANDS

soft, kindest hands,
strong, sure, deft, soft,
grace my face,
on mouth they linger.
suns, in her eyes,
that glowing amber;
blind, she is blind,
she is a vision.
though unseeing,
i see her;
she sees in me,
reach, reaches in,
tears my soul,
burns me in twain,
eyes of sun,
scorches off those moors,
soar above crows' cries,
take me with your hands,
kindest hands,
grace my face.
on mouth they linger.

M.

i have long been enamoured with amazons,
those tall, powerful warriors, dedicated to their art,
captivating men in ways they did not anticipate.

J.

there are few to whom i pledge fealty,
and fewer who galvanise me to act,
and fewer who do not desire either,
and fewer, still, similar.

AN ARGUMENT

chewed out, spit up, pinned onto the wall again;
contemplating's easy it's the thoughts that make it hard;
chances are the new alignment is what's galvanising odysseys
countering the mind, it seems; ready, steady, go into the
challenge and run with the wind, match its speed and hope
celestial forces do agree with every decision you might make;
compromising soundlessly's not always a surrender;
countering ferociously's not the only test of strength.

DREAMS

what's to remember?
can you recall it,
the beauty of a thousand stars,
a soft rain upon us;

what's there to remember?
can you recall it,
an infinite smile,
a pleasant tear in space;

to see our dream
so easily wrought,
to unlearn all
the hate we're taught
by hearts much more
broken than we
who dream to dream,
who dream to see.

CL.

admittedly, the first meeting
shattered my conceptualisations of mortality;
for so long i thought myself the sole immortal
surviving the throes of the dark,
clamouring my way from the depths
of an insatiable void.

I KNOW THEM TOO

twinkling in amber eyes
are thoughts as vast as summer skies
which are about as far away
as her mind this morn.
with the flair of auroras,
those gorgeous electronic storms,
she holds her palm to face the sun
and revels in its warmth.
her feet, although lethargic, move
with mesmerising fleetness;
the nimbleness in her dance belies
her clumsy, nervous smile.
she asked if she moved prettily;
i replied, "i cannot see the sun;"
she gasped and smote my shoulder;
i grinned; i'd meant,

"indeed.
you're glamorous and radiant,
you're clever and so filled with wit;
you must be Pallas Athene, my dear;
your mind must be a spear."

JO.

sometimes we fall for our shadows,
darker reflections, they.
it's harder to love you for yourself
than it is to love yourself vicariously.
i read this in the Mirror,
i saw it on the wall,
a note that i had left myself,
before i ran to fall.

TESLA

your name and mine are similar.
they bring to mind the thought of light,
of acts whose goals are to shine bright,
to allow humans to see at night,
to share, to share, to share.

our natures, too, might thus compare.
reclusive, though shining in a room,
intolerant, though of different things,
artistic, though of variant means;
demanding more from human beings.

VANITY

i'm told the sea's lonely again,
staring at the moon, but then,
depending which ones you follow, the scene itself is Vanity;
let it depend on gravity,
not the strange non-magnetism
which keeps the waves from touching sky,
but that which makes one run from dying.

what a strange thing regret must be,
to cause humanity to flee,
to chase after the strong desire
to set things right, fix misery.

what nightmares it must galvanise.
i gaze upon my own demise
with wistful, watchful, wary eyes.

FUTURE

i've seen
a desert culminate, the scene
took root,
decimation does not mean clean,
and i found
in deepest darkness, all their hearts,
tossed aside, a sacrifice no one needed,
despite their claims advice was heeded —

"perhaps we listened to the void
expecting a return;
perhaps we didn't know the void
had nothing in its grasp;
perhaps we thought the void
was something we could not escape;
we looked and saw only ourselves.

what calamity.
what catastrophe.
what demise;

we sought for clarity,
not for cacophony,
what we found, instead,
rendered us wise;

although at the end of things,
we might burn off all our wings,
let our desecrated bodies
clatter to the ground;

affix to us our puppet strings,
despite what our yearning brings —
our hearts may scream,
will you (please) ignore the sound."

THE END OF THINGS

can you only hear the wind blow
when we run, when we run,
or can you hear the world speed by?
do you only hear the wind blow
when we run, oh, when we run,
or can you hear the world speed by?

i see the trees, rising high,
green leaves waving in the sun,
here it is, oh, here it is: Paradise.
unthreatened by the sea,
where's the world watching?
can you see it as the clouds go,
as the clouds go by;
can you see it all fade away, oh;
do you understand the willow
as it stoops its head to cry?

can you only hear the wind blow
when we run, when we run,
or can you hear the world speed by?

do you only hear the wind blow
when we run, oh, when we run,
or can you hear the world speed by?

as we stand here,
'neath the shadow
of a highway aimed to nowhere,
as we walk beneath a sun
whose ending is assured?
can you only hear the wind blow,
or will you focus on the waves,
of the glittering sea,
of the world gone by?

GRETA

the most daring person in that room was Greta,
i'm certain that it's known;
the way she plead her case that day
is how we must our own;
and Artemisa, too, reminds all
the forests are ablaze,
that every continent with trees
must fight off greed, always;
and Mari also represents
the wellness of our earth,
for Nature is not just the trees
but all who tread her girth;
and Tekanang, of Tuvalu,
if only he could choose,
would ensure the safety of his home
which to oceans he might lose.

it's sad to see the youth incensed,
to see them all outcry;
it's shameful seeing the old smile
and, through their grimace, lie.

A SONG FOR EVERY SUN
I'VE SEEN

for every sun i've seen thus far,
a song, a song for you,
it flows forth from my heart to yours,
and though you may not hear it yet,
for time is but our distant points,
i sing for you and every sun,
for every sun, a song;

i sing it in the evenings when
you stumble down to bed,
and when you rise just after me,
i might hum it instead
(for others in my home may sleep
much longer than us two),
for every sun i've seen thus far,
a song, a song for you;

i sing it hoping that you might
receive the tune someday,
that it falls into your mind,
and much like ocean spray
finds it way from clever eyes

to those fingertips of yours,
which will then relay
my abject, heartfelt scores;

for every sun i've seen thus far
a song, a song for you;
i sing a song for every sun,
for every sun, a song.

IN HER EYES, A FOREST

in her eyes dwells a forest
always reaching for skies,
a wood as ancient and wise
as the mountains ever-looming,
as the seas which dwell beyond.

in her eyes dwells a forest
nurturing by composition,
kept well-moistened by the rain

(which falls oh-so-often,
at least every evening,
when the sun's setting, drenching
the sky in clearest crimson,
reminding clouds of pain).

in her eyes dwells a forest,
such a deep, longing green,
a hue so splendidly inviting
it devours me.

BREATHTAKING

today i've experienced the very definition of BREATHTAKING:

when her eyes, her smile wrenched me from an atmosphere

and hurled my paralysed frame into the Void.
i felt like Dorian Grey; i clung to the Self trapped within.
i could not speak. i was the portrait of bewilderment.
every attempt to breathe, to refill my deflated lungs, futile.
i reminded my heart to beat, to beat, to beat, to beat.

HORIZONS

sun, as it sets,
the skies creak, groan,
hiss; horizon shuts.
moon arises.

stars, twinkle ere;
they wonder why
they go; far, they go.
far they dwell.
far they seem.
and yet their songs
tickle my skin,
keep me breathing.

sun, as it rose,
the skies hum, sigh,
gasp; horizon shuts.
moon subsides.

PATHETIC.

it seems to me that i'll be listlessly waiting quite awhile
for someone whose heart matches mine
and mind has equal guile,
tactfully returning my witticisms easily
and chasing after every conjecture the sun could make
and then...

well, guess we'll see.
hopefully, she'll marry me.
accept a gem who's been under pressure
as sand beneath the sea,
coalesced instead of crumbling under a weight unseen;

i contemplate in metaphor, complexify analogy,
ask for no apologies from those who inconvenience me.
except, maybe, myself it seems;
from me i might expect the most.
try to be as perfect as even the holiest of ghosts.
within remains a catholic who argues with an old rabbi,
waxing philosophic with the alchemist-king inside my mind.
it feels divine, this strangest trine.
blissful as an evening spent on oceanside.

for more on those, i merely ought
to look within your eyes,
but doing so would cataclyse my soul
and send me to the skies

below which we reside with glee for a smaller eternity
than that which our own soul will know,
than that for which our sun will glow,
for less a time than we shall see,
for less a time than Earth shall be —
and yet we find vast swaths of mirth
despite the oath sworn us since birth,
a promise which to some seems cold
and instigates in others bold
urge and will that'll wax and wane
and put us all through so much pain —

but such is life, and life will be;
living's a verb; and being free.
they must be done, or else they'll cease,
leaving you sans vie, deceased.

THESES

WE WRITE WHAT WE KNOW; THE REST IS IMAGINATION

DRUGS HELP SOMETIMES,
BUT THEY ARE NEVER THE SOLE SOLUTION

LOVE WILL ALWAYS COST FAR LESS
THAN ANY FORM OF APATHY

NOT ABSOLUTE; ONE STRUGGLES TO SURVIVE IN KELVINS

THE UNITED STATES GOVERNMENT
HAS MADE ITS FATHER PROUD

ON RELATIVITY

HOW OFTEN ART SUFFERS AT THE HANDS
OF THE PATRIARCHY

THE SEA, ALWAYS CALLING — FIRST MOVEMENT

CURIOSITY IS THE URGE AND WILLINGNESS
TO EXPLORE A GREATER NARRATIVE

THE MOON, ALWAYS RISING — SECOND MOVEMENT

THEY SHOWED ME MEANING, SELF-WORTH, AND
VIBRANCE.
WITHOUT THEM, I WOULD NOT WRITE

THERE IS ALWAYS TIME FOR LOVE;
TO SHOW IT IS SIMPLE BUT REQUIRES DEDICATION

IF WE RUN FROM THAT WHICH WE DO NOT UNDERSTAND,
WE SHALL SOON FIND NO PLACE TO HIDE

A GOVERNMENT, SOCIETY, A PERSON WHO DOES NOT
CHERISH ALL PEOPLE CONDEMNS AND CONFINES ALL

TO FILL A VOID WITH NOTHINGNESS
IS TO PRAY FOR SELF-DESTRUCTION

THE RAIN, ALWAYS FALLING — THIRD MOVEMENT

AUTHOR'S NOTE:

when reading *THESES*, the intended experience
is to have the title read as the last line of the poem.

WE WRITE WHAT WE KNOW;
THE REST IS IMAGINATION

Of love and romance I am scared to write
for I write of things experienced;
I see love's many forms,
remember from ages past,
my dreams within dreams,
my favourite spectre, romance,
the legends and myths,
the sacrifices, compromises,
endless dance, stumbles,
the affections and affectations,
accents and accentuations,
rare modern day implementations
of love and romance, of
the willingness to put someone forth
as much as oneself — not before, nor after,
matching pace for pace,
hands held and whispers shared —
what know I of love, for I have yet to live it?

DRUGS HELP SOMETIMES, BUT THEY ARE NEVER THE SOLE SOLUTION

Psychologists have yet to find
that spectre called the mind.
they only find that which
implies its existence, the aftereffects,
much as our sole awareness of breezes
are our relief or displeasure as they pass;
sometimes hurricanes, moist and expedient,
sometimes warm, soft, and tender.

Psychiatrists employ their pills and injections
as engineers would design ships —
by amending the mechanisms, one might
make a canoe a battleship,
a leaking oil tanker into a currach.
how the wind affects these is indeed
dependent in part upon the dimensions.

Psychologists adjust the sails,
retie frayed knots; teach a woman to sail,
she will command a fleet.

LOVE WILL ALWAYS COST
LESS THAN ANY FORM OF
APATHY

But it is hard to not know love
when you see it everywhere you look,
in the sunflowers aspiring for celestial illumination,
in the bees hovering amongst the flowers,
in the slow blinks of saccharine cats,
in the colours of a sunrise,
in the optimism of a sunset, of parting clouds,
in the sea returning to shore,
in a puppy's softest snore,
in the laughter of crows,
in the darling of foxes and dragonflies,
in the glittering of rivers rushing,
in the light reaching through leaves
to softly caress your upturned face.

NOT ABSOLUTE; ONE STRUGGLES TO SURVIVE IN KELVINS

When I imagine our hands intertwined
as we waltz beneath the softly falling snow,
that delicate barrage of chill
rendered inert and intangible by the
warmth exuding from our synchronised hearts,
our quiet breaths, our clasped hands,
the warmth of love keeping warm
even me, whose natural barrier against chill
is so impotent you tease me by
pleading, mischievous glint in your glittering eye,
to fetch you ice for your beverage
whenever you get the chance.
of course I repay you
by clasping my frigid hands
to your divinely warm face;
I remark upon the rising of hot air;
you snap your teeth at my fingers.
by fire? By ice?
love is the fine, glorious middle.

THE UNITED STATES GOVERNMENT HAS MADE ITS FATHER PROUD

Upon the news is tyranny,
a thousand masks it wears.
people who claim to love their neighbours
so obviously despise themselves.
begging for the end, they are,
hoping that it comes —
a death cult, a death cult they have become,
concerned only with After, with
an end they do not know.
to callously crusade against every Other
is the gravest sin.
life is not a tackling game;
there is no team to win.
the spread of Western Europe
has razed a thousand grounds;
the hatred of all species,
from tenth as many crowns.
no matter hue nor orientation,
in blood the world will drown.

ON RELATIVITY

The idea of dying is not unfamiliar to me.
of my 2.5 decades,
I have imagined it since I was a fifth my age.
I discovered it upon
waking from a dream
in the back of my mother's Saturn.
the ratio of time experienced:
to a five-year-old,
two hours is much more
than to the twenty-five year old.
one day is one of five(three hundred sixty-five).
twenty-four hours is nothingness to an adult.
to a child, it is an eternity.

Einstein regards imagination as the
greatest processor of reality.
eternities exist in seconds should you
pinch the screen and spread,
zoom in, closer, closer.
the less space taken,
the greater time to fill.

We are ladybirds' immortals.
no wonder depression's unspoken side effect
is a greater sense of time;
we who drown in melancholy —
not drown; float, hang;
to drown is to at least do something —
are compressed, squashed into
miniscule, unrecognisable bits,
data, tinged in colourlessness.
every moment is a chore.

A recent study found that
procrastination is always justified.
there is always a reason.
laziness does not exist.
productivity is not the reason for living.
your value is much like dividing by zero:
our current metrics cannot determine them;
skyward reaching, undefined.

HOW OFTEN ART SUFFERS
AT THE HANDS OF THE
PATRIARCHY

I keep a poster of Marilyn Monroe
sitting on the floor in the corner
of my bedroom, opposite my
replica of Michelangelo I made
in eighth grade.
I like to imagine that they
comprehend each other.
Marilyn covers her mouth with
glittering, sequinned gloves;
we all know the power of her smile.
why would anyone obscure it?
I remember reading how smiles
are but a socialised form of
revealing one's fangs, a vestige
of more feral days;

"I will not bite you," we beam,
an oath of friendliness. An invitation.
Marilyn invited the whole world in.
too few thanked her for the party.
fewer, still, recognised her there.
few, if any, saw her.

And the sculptor? He carved
such angels free. Angels, those
terrifying, massive, incomprehensible things.
how many blisters torn open, how many
nights crying over bleeding, shaking
hands, how many evenings did Michelangelo
pray for his penance to be at end?
he loved men who could not love him.
to love as he was sin, doom.
could his God forgive him if he
loosed his messengers from their
marble, brutal, veiny tombs?
could he find God's mercy tucked
away in stone, chisel his name
into God's cold, smooth heart?
could he paint his way into heaven?
"Let God be there," he dreamed.

THE SEA, ALWAYS CALLING –
FIRST MOVEMENT

The sea is always calling.
saline-teared mother from whom
all life is ushered,
she who holds the heat
which would obliterate us.
before land, there was endless sea,
and from her was ushered – cessed
to us – land; from her depths
we crawled, upwards and onwards.
all good others wish their children
to surpass them, to grow beyond,
to aspire and inspire, to be.
but the sea is always calling,
that fantastic and unfathomable depth,
a reflection of the cosmos above.
she reassures us, gently waving,
always reminding us of
our days upon and before the shore.

CURIOSITY IS THE URGE AND WILLINGNESS TO EXPLORE A GREATER NARRATIVE

Of those things without which
I would find the world devoid
of value, there are three:
is there a sky above us?
is there bread to eat?
is there, somewhere,
even if it is not me,
someone falling in love?
of the most vital things to us,
foremost, one may say, is
sunlight. Others water.
others gravity. Electromagnetism.
some say gods, whichever
variation they praise beyond themselves.
before themselves.
English is overwhelmed by misunderstanding;
the Irish had it right.
in English, there are gods of things.
English is all about dominion, you know.

control, control, control.
everyone else knows their gods are not of
anything.
their power stems not from
manipulation, from reins.
English gods are inferior; they
control, and thus have things
to lose.
everyone else's gods merely are.
The English still think
Adam could be plurality;
America thinks it was first to split the Adam,
when it was perfected in Hebrew
before the word "god" even existed.

THE MOON, ALWAYS RISING
– SECOND MOVEMENT

And I saw,
walking softly, you,
deep in thought, introspective,
your eyes philosophic deluge.
"hello," you waved
framed in the gold
of sunrise, of morning,
and I smiled to you.
and you, you did
remind me of
that oldest question
that my thoughts
had subdued.

for you, framed in the gold
of sunrise, of morning,
shared what you knew.
in the darkness
lies an aegis, gleaming bright,
the moon that shines,
even unseen,
is always rising.

THEY SHOWED ME MEANING,
SELF-WORTH, AND
VIBRANCY. WITHOUT THEM,
I WOULD NOT WRITE.

Perhaps foremost, I must thank Mucha.
he showed me the intricacies of meaning,
the delicate interplay between myth –
those stories greater than our own,
through which we understand ourselves –
and the concreting steps of alchemy.
to put myself into the work,
I took lessons from Gentileschi,
whose fearlessness and conviction
did not merely show in her brushstrokes,
but in the eyes of her subject herself,
in the furrows of her brow.
I understood her story before I knew it.
of finding wonders in the world and relaying
the pricelessness of the cosmos
to those who counted pennies,
of revealing the vibrancy of a world taken for granted,
Vincent taught me most.

THERE IS ALWAYS TIME FOR LOVE; TO SHOW IT IS SIMPLE BUT REQUIRES DEDICATION

I think of love,
I think of love
when sunlight dances across a wave,
I think of love,
I think of love
when the grasses lean in softer breeze,
I think of love,
I think of love
when the stars glitter round pristine moon,
I think of love,
I think of love
when laughs fill teashops more than steaming cups,

I think of love,
I think of love
when coals pop and warm up the den,
I think of love,
I think of love
when children tell of their playthings' lives,
I think of love,
I think of love
when cloudless skies bring bows made of rain.

IF WE RUN FROM WHAT WE
DO NOT UNDERSTAND, WE
SHALL SOON FIND NO PLACE
TO HIDE

Of a rose-hued moon
I feel such jubilation;
embrace of two goddesses,
divine inspiration.
on the face is dear Artemis,
blushing as Eos nears her;
I often do wonder
if they'd whisper of me.
I don't want an answer,
I'll just stand here, watching,
as Huntress and mother
to the great Hesperides
catch up on their distance,
reigning over variant skies,
temporal dissolution
defied with great glee.
there's nothing more powerful
than two wanderers embracing;

why do people find terror
in such beautiful things
as two women embracing,
as two men still, kissing,
as all different cultures,
tongues and accents and hues,
as neurodivergence,
as the youth and the older,
and this planet, here, too.

A GOVERNMENT, SOCIETY, A PERSON WHO DOES NOT CHERISH ALL PEOPLE CONDEMNS AND CONFINES ALL

The looming summer's heat,
its perfumes overflowing with
wanderlust, the incessant
craving for adventure
in the ways vampires crave blood,
that essence which was known
and overabundant in their youth,
now absent and yearned
with the intensity of
unbridled summer sun,
that piercing and unyielding thing,
that celestial rapier —
this invigorates that drive for exploration
embedded in my soul.

"Out!" my soul screams,
my blood rushes,
my mind flies, "Out!"
I remember how many who look like me,
who could have been me,
were killed by men and governments
demanding them to be shut "Out!"
locked "Out!" put "Out!"
kept "Out!"

When living is made a crime,
only death is absolution.
the only mode of survival
becomes abnegation.
they would collapse us into
a nothingness so inherent that
no light could escape.
they make of us a singularity.
I sigh, and close my door again.

TO FILL A VOID WITH NOTHINGNESS IS TO PRAY FOR SELF-DESTRUCTION

We're always astonished,
hyperbolically polished
by the mirth that's abolished
by all of these revenants
hunting and killing
and all the blood spilling
is this what God's willing?
I really don't want it,
this world that's so haunted
by have-its who flaunt it,
leaving us taunted —
are we not the majority?
what do they want from me?
where is equality?
why is it they're hating me?
what have I done to thee?

I merely was born
and you call me adversary.
does the rain not too fall on we
who exist on this planet,
does it not fall down equally?
why hate humanity?
why not instead
formulate green urbanity,
quell the disparity,
cataclyse hunger, live
a life so responsibly
it invokes in land and sea
only growth and good quality
air so we all may breathe.
we could stop animosity
based on sexuality,
colour and creed,
and this putrid mediocrity
on which the world's settled,
and order long peddled
by the spiteful and selfish,
by those always seeking
what peace they lack within.

THE RAIN, ALWAYS FALLING
– THIRD MOVEMENT

Looked up to the sky
and the beauty I see
as water pours down
washing fury from me,
the joy and the shock
of a plan gone awry,
beheld is the mercy
of the afternoon light
as rain ushers forth
landing on toe and face –
the water that flies
will be gently replaced –
and life runs its course
as a hare on the field;
to Cosmos themselves
I am ready to yield;
no thunder relaying
distances far nor near,
no lightning in sight
but the lingering fear

of electrons in motion
striking us from the sky
as if old Perun
really wants us to die,
and Kabeyesi!
to the young Fire King,
whose multi-hued wife
gales and lightning strike brings,

and don't we all scurry
when the Thunderbird sings
as fret climbs our cheeks
and our corneas sting
its oddly shaped needle
urging from our eyes
a similar water
to that one which flies
upwards and on breezes
coaxed up by the sun,
condensed by the coolness
of the generous one
who keeps in some heat
and of others lets go
ensuring survival
and perpetual flow —
an oath that was sworn
well before we were born,
a promise well-kept
despite being so worn
ragged and ruthlessly

a puncture was torn;
perhaps of their tears,
perhaps their release
explains all these raindrops
always falling...

Though some proved sharper in recoil than others,
I am glad to have collided with every one of you.
Thank you.
S

Sólfjodur is a founding member of the Sólkráka Collective. They are the resident poet and storykeeper, and much prefer to stay in the relative safety of their library than traverse the cosmos as their chronically displaced partner does.